INTRODUCTION

Mixers and blenders make cooking easier and much more fun. They dispense with all the laborious tasks and allow you to achieve far more in much less time.

If you use a mixer you can forget chores like whisking, beating and rubbing in mixtures; and the blender will make you smooth soups, fruit purées, breadcrumbs, baby foods and drinks. It can even chop parsley and dry ingredients like nuts!

The problems of unexpected guests arriving or the family descending on you for the weekend will vanish, as there are so many exciting recipes you can make in a matter of minutes. Delicious soups, pâtés, sauces and cakes can easily be prepared with the flick of a switch.

And, remember, don't hide your mixer or blender away in a kitchen cupboard – keep it out ready and waiting on the work surface and you'll find you use it almost every day for all sorts of delicious dishes!

MIXERS

Most mixers have different blades for different jobs. As a general rule, use the beater for heavier creamed mixtures and the whisk for light mixtures, like whisked sponges.

If your mixer has a choice of speeds, use a slow speed for rubbed-in mixtures, medium speed for creamed mixtures and maximum speed for egg whites, soufflés and sponges.

Large Table Mixers: These can cope with large quantities and have a greater speed variation than the smaller models. They can be used for rubbing in, creaming, whisking and kneading. Different blades are provided for each job; most models include a dough hook, a whisk and a basic beater.

Hand Mixers: These can be used to carry out most of the tasks a table mixer does but they have a smaller capacity. A hand mixer cannot cope with bread dough, fruit cake mixtures or almond paste. Most models have three speeds.

An advantage of the hand mixer is that it can be used in any bowl. Except for lightweight hand mixers, most models have a detachable stand and bowl. Lightweight models should not be used for pastry or biscuits.

BLENDERS

These are available as free-standing models, with their own motor unit, and as attachments to the larger hand mixers and table mixers. Heavy mixtures such as pâtés and spreads can be made in larger blenders only.

Most blenders have a choice of three speeds. If you have a model which operates on one speed, adjust the blender timings accordingly: blend for a shorter time if the recipe states slow speed; slightly longer if it states high speed.

6

USING THE MIXER/BLENDER

Mixers and blenders are ideal for preparing food in bulk. Fruit purées are quick and easy to prepare in batches in the blender and freeze well. They are then ready as a base for a fool, mousse or ice cream, or to serve as a sauce.

It is just as easy to prepare 1½ lb shortcrust pastry as it is to make 8 oz when using a mixer. Simply freeze the remainder or wrap in a plastic bag and store in the refrigerator for up to 4 days. Similarly 2 sponges can be mixed as quickly as one, so double the quantity and freeze one of them.

Breadcrumbs can be quickly made in the blender from fresh or stale bread. Cut the bread into cubes, switch on the motor and drop the cubes through the hole in the lid. It is easier to make a small quantity at a time. If your blender does not have a hole in the lid, just put the cubes of bread into the goblet and blend for a few seconds.

Care and Cleaning: Always read the manufacturer's instructions to check the operating procedures, the quantities that the machine will cope with and the type of food that can be prepared. Do not prepare more food than the maximum quantity recommended as over-loading the machine can damage the motor.

After use, wipe the machine with a cloth that has been wrung out in hot soapy water, then dry thoroughly. Never use abrasives or allow the motor to get wet. Wash the mixer bowl and beaters in detergent and dry thoroughly.

The blender is best cleaned by placing a little hot water in the goblet with a drop of liquid detergent. Cover with the lid and run for a few seconds. Rinse well, drain and dry.

Shortcrust Pastry

250 g (8 oz) plain
 flour, sifted
pinch of salt
125 g (4 oz) butter
 or margarine, cut
 into pieces
2 tablespoons water

Place the flour, salt and fat in the mixer bowl. Mix on slow speed, increasing to medium speed, until the mixture resembles breadcrumbs. Add the water and mix on slow speed just long enough to bind the ingredients together. Turn onto a floured surface and knead lightly until smooth. Chill for 15 minutes.

Makes 250 g (8 oz) pastry

VARIATIONS:

Wholemeal Pastry: Replace the plain flour with wholemeal flour.

Cheese Pastry: Sift ½ teaspoon dry mustard and a pinch of cayenne pepper with the flour and salt. Add 75 g (3 oz) grated Cheddar cheese with the water.

Rich Shortcrust Pastry

175 g (6 oz) plain
 flour, sifted
75 g (3 oz) butter,
 cut into pieces
25 g (1 oz) caster
 sugar
1 egg yolk
1 tablespoon iced
 water

Place the flour, butter and sugar in the mixer bowl. Mix on slow speed, increasing to medium speed, until the mixture resembles breadcrumbs. Add the egg yolk and water and mix on slow speed just long enough to bind the mixture together. Turn onto a floured surface and knead lightly until smooth. Chill for 15 minutes.

Makes 175 g (6 oz) pastry

Choux Pastry

50 g (2 oz) butter or
 margarine
150 ml (¼ pint)
 water
65 g (2½ oz) plain
 flour, sifted
2 eggs, beaten

Melt the fat in a saucepan, add the water and bring to the boil. Remove from the heat, add the flour all at once and beat well with a wooden spoon until the mixture leaves the side of the pan clean. Place in the mixer bowl and add the eggs a little at a time, beating at slow speed. Turn to high speed and beat for 1 minute.

Makes a '2-egg quantity' pastry

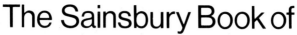

The Sainsbury Book of
MIXER & BLENDER COOKING
Carole Handslip

CONTENTS

Soups	10
Pâtes & Mousses	18
Sauces, Dressings & Dips	28
Main Course Dishes	36
Desserts	50
Cakes, Biscuits & Breads	64
Drinks & Cocktails	82
Index	94

Published exclusively for
J Sainsbury Limited
Stamford Street, London SE1 9LL
by Cathay Books
59 Grosvenor Street, London W1

First published 1982

© Cathay Books 1982
ISBN 0 86178 130 9

Printed in Hong Kong

NOTES

Standard spoon measurements are used in all recipes
1 tablespoon = one 15 ml spoon
1 teaspoon = one 5 ml spoon.

Fresh herbs are used unless otherwise stated. If
unobtainable substitute a bouquet garni of the
equivalent dried herbs, or use dried herbs instead
but halve the quantities stated.

Use freshly ground black pepper where pepper is
specified.

If fresh yeast is unobtainable, substitute dried yeast
but use only half the recommended quantity and
follow the manufacturer's instructions for
reconstituting.

Ovens should be preheated to the specified
temperature.

For all recipes, quantities are given in both metric
and imperial measures. Follow either set but not a
mixture of both, because they are not
interchangeable.

Preparation of ingredients marked with an asterisk
is explained on pages 6-7. Basic pastry recipes are
given on page 8.

SOUPS

Cucumber and Yogurt Soup

1 cucumber, peeled
   and chopped
300 g (10 oz)
   natural low-fat
   yogurt
300 ml (½ pint)
   milk
10 mint leaves
1 small clove garlic
salt and pepper
mint sprig to
   garnish

Place all the ingredients, with salt and pepper to taste, in the blender and blend on maximum speed for 40 seconds. Chill well.

Stir well, then pour into a chilled tureen. Garnish with a mint sprig to serve.

Serves 6

Gazpacho

500 g (1 lb)
  tomatoes, skinned
1 small onion
2 cloves garlic
3 tablespoons olive
  oil
2 tablespoons wine
  vinegar
300 ml (½ pint)
  tomato juice
salt and pepper
1 cucumber, peeled
300 ml (½ pint)
  water
1 small green pepper
croûtons to serve

Chop the tomatoes, onion and garlic.
Place in the blender with the oil,
vinegar and tomato juice. Season to
taste with salt and pepper.

Roughly chop half the cucumber
and add to the blender. Blend on
maximum speed for 30 seconds.
Pour into a tureen, add the water and
chill the soup in the refrigerator.

Dice the remaining cucumber and
the green pepper, discarding the core
and seeds. Place in small bowls. Put
the croûtons in another small bowl.
Serve with the chilled gazpacho.

Serves 6

Cream of Watercress Soup

2 bunches watercress,
  chopped
2 tablespoons oil
1 onion, chopped
1 tablespoon plain
  flour
900 ml (1½ pints)
  hot milk
salt and pepper
150 ml (¼ pint)
  single cream

Reserve a few watercress sprigs for garnish. Heat the oil in a pan, add the onion and watercress, cover and cook gently for 6 minutes. Stir in the flour, then the milk and salt and pepper. Cover and simmer for 20 minutes.

Cool slightly, then blend on maximum speed for 30 seconds. Return to the pan, stir in the cream and heat gently. Pour into individual warmed bowls and garnish with watercress.
Serves 4

Artichoke Soup

2 tablespoons oil
1 large onion,
  chopped
500 g (1 lb) Jerusalem
  artichokes, chopped
600 ml (1 pint) light
  stock or water
salt and pepper
300 ml (½ pint)
  milk
1 teaspoon lemon
  juice
TO GARNISH:
single cream
chopped parsley

Heat the oil in a pan, add the onion and cook until softened. Add the artichokes and cook for 5 minutes. Add the stock or water, and salt and pepper to taste. Bring to the boil, cover and simmer for 40 minutes.

Cool slightly, then blend on maximum speed for 30 seconds. Return to the pan, add the milk and lemon juice and reheat. Pour into individual warmed bowls. Swirl a spoonful of cream on top of each bowl and sprinkle with parsley.
Serves 4

Avocado Soup

1 large avocado pear
450 ml (¾ pint) milk
150 g (5 oz) natural
  low-fat yogurt
½ teaspoon grated
  onion
1 teaspoon lemon
  juice
½ teaspoon Worcester-
  shire sauce
salt and pepper
TO GARNISH:
single cream
chopped chives

Peel the avocado, halve and remove the stone. Cut into chunks and place in the blender with the remaining ingredients, adding salt and pepper to taste. Blend on maximum speed for 30 seconds. Pour into individual soup bowls and chill.

Swirl a spoonful of cream on top of each bowl and sprinkle with chives to serve.
Serves 4

Potato and Onion Soup

2 tablespoons oil
1 large onion,
  chopped
250 g (8 oz)
  potatoes, chopped
600 ml (1 pint) stock
1 clove garlic
1 bay leaf
salt and pepper
300 ml (½ pint)
  milk
chopped parsley to
  garnish

Heat the oil in a large pan, add the onion and potatoes and cook for 5 minutes until softened. Add the stock, garlic, bay leaf, and salt and pepper to taste. Cover and simmer gently for 30 minutes.

Cool slightly, remove the bay leaf and blend on maximum speed for 30 seconds.

Return to the pan with the milk and reheat. Pour into a warmed tureen and sprinkle with parsley.
Serves 4

Cream of Spinach Soup

2 tablespoons oil
1 onion, chopped
1 tablespoon
    wholemeal flour
600 ml (1 pint) light
    stock or water
1/4 teaspoon grated
    nutmeg
salt and pepper
500 g (1 lb) spinach
squeeze of lemon
    juice
284 ml (10 fl oz)
    single cream
croûtons to serve

Heat the oil in a large pan, add the onion and cook gently for 5 minutes until softened. Mix in the flour then add the stock or water, nutmeg, and salt and pepper to taste. Bring to the boil, stirring, then add the spinach. Cover and simmer for 20 minutes.

Cool slightly, then blend on maximum speed for 30 seconds. Return the soup to the pan. Add the lemon juice and 200 ml (1/3 pint) of the cream. Check the seasoning, then pour into a warmed tureen. Swirl the remaining cream on top of the soup, using a fork. Serve with croûtons.
Serves 4

Tomato Soup

2 tablespoons oil
1 carrot, chopped
1 small onion,
    chopped
1 celery stick,
    chopped
500 g (1 lb)
    tomatoes, skinned
    and chopped
1 clove garlic,
    chopped
1 bay leaf
1 tablespoon tomato
    purée
750 ml (1 1/4 pints)
    light stock or
    water
2 teaspoons caster
    sugar
TO FINISH:
chopped chives
croûtons

Heat the oil in a large pan, add the carrot, onion and celery and cook for 5 minutes until softened. Add the tomatoes, garlic, bay leaf, tomato purée and stock or water. Cover and simmer gently for 30 minutes.

Cool slightly, remove the bay leaf and blend on maximum speed for 30 seconds.

Return the soup to the pan and stir in the sugar. Reheat gently, then pour into a warmed tureen. Sprinkle with chives and serve with croûtons.
Serves 4

Country Vegetable Soup

1 carrot
1 onion
1 potato
1 celery stick
4 parsley sprigs
900 ml (1½ pints)
  stock or water
1 teaspoon salt
½ teaspoon pepper

Chop the vegetables roughly and place in the blender with the parsley and 600 ml (1 pint) of the stock or water. Blend on maximum speed for 8 seconds to chop the vegetables finely.

Pour into a saucepan, add the remaining stock or water, salt and pepper. Cover and simmer for 30 minutes. Pour into individual soup bowls to serve.

Serves 4

Pea Soup

1 carrot
2 celery sticks
1 onion
2 mint sprigs
1.2 litres (2 pints)
  stock
250 g (8 oz) dried
  peas, soaked
  overnight
300 ml (½ pint)
  milk
salt and pepper
1 tablespoon chopped
  mint to garnish

Roughly chop the carrot, celery and onion. Place all the ingredients except the milk in a large saucepan, seasoning with salt and pepper to taste. Bring to the boil, cover and simmer very gently for 2 to 3 hours, until the peas are tender.

Cool slightly, then blend half the soup on maximum speed for 30 seconds. Repeat with the other half. Return the soup to the pan, add the milk and reheat. Pour into a warmed tureen and sprinkle with the mint.

Serves 6

Lentil and Vegetable Soup

2 tablespoons oil
1 leek, chopped
1 onion, chopped
1 carrot, chopped
1 clove garlic,
  chopped
175 g (6 oz) lentils
900 ml (1½ pints)
  light stock or
  water
4 parsley sprigs
salt and pepper
1 tablespoon chopped
  parsley to garnish

Heat the oil in a large pan. Add the leek, onion, carrot and garlic and fry until softened. Add the remaining ingredients, with salt and pepper to taste. Bring to the boil, cover and simmer for 45 minutes, stirring occasionally.

Allow the soup to cool slightly, then blend on maximum speed for 30 seconds.

Return to the pan and reheat gently. Pour into a warmed tureen and sprinkle with the parsley.

Serves 4 to 6

PATES & MOUSSES

Sardine Pâté

2 x 120 g (4¼ oz)
  cans sardines in
  oil, drained
113 g (4 oz) cream
  cheese
2 tablespoons lemon
  juice
4 parsley sprigs
90 ml (3 fl oz)
  soured cream

TO GARNISH:
parsley sprig

Place the sardines, cream cheese, lemon juice, parsley and soured cream in the blender and blend on maximum speed for 30 seconds.

Spoon into a small bowl and garnish with parsley. Serve with rye bread (see page 79).

Serves 4

Smoked Mackerel Terrine

350 g (12 oz)
   smoked mackerel
113 g (4 oz) cream
   cheese
25 g (1 oz) butter,
   melted
1 teaspoon lemon
   juice
4 tablespoons single
   cream
salt and pepper
TO GARNISH:
lemon twist
fennel sprigs

Remove the skin and bones from the
fish and cut 125 g (4 oz) of the flesh
into finger-length pieces. Place the
remaining fish in the blender with
the rest of the ingredients, adding
salt and pepper to taste. Blend on
medium speed until smooth; turn off
the blender occasionally and scrape
the unblended fish onto the blades.

Place half the mixture in an
earthenware terrine and arrange the
pieces of fish on top. Cover with the
remaining mixture, smoothing the
top evenly. Chill until required.

Garnish with a lemon twist and
fennel sprigs and serve with toast.
Serves 6 to 8

Pork and Thyme Terrine

4-6 large rashers
  streaky bacon,
  derinded
350 g (12 oz)
  ground pork
250 g (8 oz) pigs'
  liver, minced
125 g (4 oz) pork
  sausage meat
1 onion, finely
  chopped
1 clove garlic, crushed
1 teaspoon chopped
  thyme
1 tablespoon chopped
  parsley
salt and pepper

Line a 500 g (1 lb) loaf tin with the bacon. Place remaining ingredients in the mixer bowl, adding salt and pepper to taste. Mix on medium speed.

Place in the tin, smoothing the top evenly. Cover with foil.

Place in a roasting pan half-filled with water and cook in a preheated moderate oven, 160°C (325°F), Gas Mark 3, for 1¼ to 1½ hours. Replace foil with greaseproof paper.

Place a 1 kg (2 lb) weight on top and leave until cold. Chill overnight then turn onto a serving dish. Serve with toast as a starter, or salad as a main course.

Serves 6 to 10

Farmhouse Terrine

500 g (1 lb) large
  rashers streaky
  bacon, derinded
250 g (8 oz) pigs'
  liver, minced
250 g (8 oz) minced
  veal
1 onion, minced
125 g (4 oz)
  wholemeal bread,
  cubed
few parsley sprigs
1 egg
1 clove garlic,
  crushed
salt and pepper
1 bay leaf

Stretch the bacon rashers with a palette knife. Line a 900 ml (1½ pint) terrine with one third of the bacon rashers and set aside a further one third of them. Mince the remaining bacon and place in the mixer bowl with the liver, veal and onion.

Place the bread and parsley in the blender and blend on medium speed for 30 seconds. Add to the meats with the egg, garlic, and salt and pepper to taste. Mix on medium speed.

Spread half of the mixture in the terrine evenly and press firmly. Place 2 to 3 bacon rashers on top and cover with the remaining mixture. Finish with a layer of the remaining rashers.

Place a bay leaf on top and cover with the lid. Place in a roasting pan half-filled with water. Cook in a pre-heated moderate oven, 160°C (325°F), Gas Mark 3, for 1½ to 1¾ hours.

Remove the lid, place a 1 kg (2 lb) weight on top and leave until cold. Serve chilled, with toast or salad.

Serves 8 to 10

Greek Aubergine Pâté

2 large aubergines
1 clove garlic,
   chopped
1 tablespoon wine
   vinegar
2 tablespoons olive
   oil
salt and pepper
2 tomatoes, skinned,
   seeded and finely
   chopped
1 small onion, finely
   chopped
TO GARNISH:
few lettuce leaves
tomato slices
onion rings
black olives

Prick the aubergines all over with a fork, cut in half and place cut side down on a greased baking sheet. Bake in a preheated moderately hot oven, 190°C (375°F), Gas Mark 5, for 30 to 40 minutes until the aubergines are soft and the skins are black.

Remove the skins from the aubergines and place the flesh in the blender with the garlic, vinegar and oil, seasoning with salt and pepper to taste. Blend on maximum speed for 1 minute until smooth. Stir in the tomatoes and onion.

Arrange the pâté on a bed of lettuce on a serving dish. Garnish with tomato slices, onion rings and olives and serve with French bread.
Serves 6

Hummous

75 g (3 oz) chick
   peas, soaked
   overnight
2 tablespoons tahini
   (see note)
2 cloves garlic
grated rind and juice
   of ½ lemon
3 tablespoons olive
   oil
salt and pepper
chopped parsley to
   garnish

Drain the chick peas, place in a pan and cover with cold water. Bring to the boil and simmer gently for 2 to 2½ hours until the peas are soft. Drain and reserve 4 tablespoons of the liquid.

Place the peas in the blender with the reserved liquid and remaining ingredients, adding salt and pepper to taste. Blend on medium speed for 30 seconds, scraping the mixture back onto the blades if necessary. Check the seasoning then place in a small bowl. Sprinkle with parsley and serve with crusty bread.
Serves 4 to 6
NOTE: Tahini is a type of sesame seed paste, obtainable from health food shops and delicatessens.

Taramasalata

75 g (3 oz) smoked
    cods' roe
3 slices bread, crusts
    removed, cubed
2 tablespoons water
juice of 1 small
    lemon
1 clove garlic,
    chopped
4 tablespoons olive
    oil
TO GARNISH:
black olives
½ lemon

Place the cods' roe, bread, water,
lemon juice and garlic in the blender
and blend on minimum speed for
30 seconds, scraping the mixture
back onto the blades if necessary.
Increase to medium speed and
gradually add the oil, as for a
mayonnaise.

Serve in a small bowl, garnished
with a slice of lemon, olives and
lemon wedges. Serve with crusty
bread.
Serves 6 to 8

Salmon Mousse

150 ml (¼ pint)
   water
15 g (½ oz) *gelatine*
1 x 212 g (7½ oz)
   can red salmon
juice of ½ lemon
142 ml (5 fl oz)
   soured cream
salt and pepper
150 ml (¼ pint)
   double cream,
   lightly whipped
175 g (6 oz)
   cucumber, peeled
   and diced
TO GARNISH:
cucumber slices or
   fennel sprigs

Place 3 tablespoons of the water in a
small saucepan, sprinkle over the
gelatine and leave for 5 minutes.
Heat gently until dissolved, then
place in the blender.

Add the salmon and its juice,
lemon juice, soured cream,
remaining water, and salt and pepper
to taste. Blend on maximum speed
for 1 minute then turn into a basin.
When just beginning to set, fold in
the cream and cucumber.

Turn into an oiled 900 ml
(1½ pint) mould and chill until set.

Turn out onto a serving dish and
garnish with cucumber or fennel.
Serve with thinly sliced, buttered
brown bread.
Serves 6

Avocado Mousse

2 avocado pears
150 g (5 oz) natural
  low-fat yogurt
150 ml (¼ pint)
  milk
15 g (½ oz) gelatine
150 ml (¼ pint)
  boiling water
1 teaspoon finely
  chopped onion
1 teaspoon lemon
  juice
1 teaspoon Worcester-
  shire sauce
salt and pepper
150 ml (¼ pint)
  double cream,
  whipped
watercress sprigs to
  garnish

Peel the avocados, halve and remove the stones. Cut the avocados into chunks and place in the blender with the yogurt and milk.

Soak the gelatine in 2 tablespoons cold water to soften. Pour the boiling water onto the gelatine and stir until dissolved, then pour into the blender. Add the onion, lemon juice, Worcestershire sauce, and salt and pepper to taste. Blend on maximum speed for 30 seconds.

Turn into a basin and leave to cool. When just beginning to thicken, fold in the cream and pour into a greased 1.2 litre (2 pint) mould. Chill until set.

Turn out onto a serving dish and garnish with watercress.
Serves 6

Potted Chicken

250 g (8 oz) cooked chicken, chopped
50 g (2 oz) cooked ham, chopped
150 g (5 oz) concentrated (or clarified) butter, melted
pinch of grated nutmeg
salt and pepper
1 bay leaf

Place half the meats, 50 g (2 oz) of the butter, the nutmeg, and salt and pepper to taste in the blender. Blend at medium speed until smooth; turn off the blender occasionally and scrape the unblended mixture back onto the blades. Transfer to a small basin.

Blend the remaining meats and 50 g (2 oz) of the butter in the same way and add to the basin. Mix well and check the seasoning.

Press into a small serving dish with the back of a spoon, smooth the surface and place the bay leaf in the centre. Pour the remaining butter over the surface to coat completely.

Leave until set, then cover with cling film and chill in the refrigerator until required.
Serves 6 to 8
NOTE: This will keep in the refrigerator for up to 4 days.

Herb and Chicken Liver Pâté

2 tablespoons oil
1 onion, chopped
250 g (8 oz) chicken
  livers
1 clove garlic, chopped
1 tablespoon chopped
  parsley
1½ teaspoons each
  chopped thyme
  and marjoram
salt and pepper
125 g (4 oz) butter,
  melted
1 tablespoon brandy
50 g (2 oz)
  concentrated (or
  clarified) butter,
  melted
parsley sprig to
  garnish

Heat the oil in a frying pan, add the onion and fry for 3 minutes until softened. Add the chicken livers, garlic, herbs, and salt and pepper to taste, and cook gently for 8 to 10 minutes. Cool slightly, then chop roughly.

Place the mixture in the blender with the ordinary butter and brandy and blend on maximum speed for 30 seconds. Transfer to a bowl, allow to cool, then beat well.

Turn into a small serving dish and smooth evenly. Pour the concentrated butter over the surface and leave until set.

Garnish with parsley and serve with toast.

Serves 6

SAUCES, DRESSINGS & DIPS

White Sauce

25 g (1 oz) butter
25 g (1 oz) plain
  flour
300 ml (½ pint) hot
  milk
salt and pepper

Place all the ingredients in the blender, seasoning with salt and pepper to taste, and blend on maximum speed for 30 seconds.

Pour into a saucepan, bring gently to the boil and cook for 2 minutes, stirring constantly.

Makes 300 ml (½ pint)

VARIATIONS:

Cheese Sauce: Stir 50 g (2 oz) grated Cheddar cheese and a pinch of mustard into the finished sauce.

Parsley Sauce: Add 15 g (½ oz) parsley (stalks removed) to the blender with the other ingredients.

Tomato Sauce

2 tablespoons olive oil
1 onion, chopped
1 clove garlic, crushed
500 g (1 lb) tomatoes, skinned and chopped
250 ml (8 fl oz) stock
2 teaspoons tomato purée
1 bay leaf
1 teaspoon soft brown sugar
salt and pepper

Heat the oil in a pan, add the onion and fry for 5 minutes until softened. Add the remaining ingredients, with salt and pepper to taste, cover and simmer for 20 minutes, stirring occasionally.

Cool slightly, remove the bay leaf and blend on maximum speed for 30 seconds. Return to the saucepan and reheat gently.

Serve with pasta, or as an accompaniment to fish dishes.
Makes 450 ml (3/4 pint)

Apple Sauce

*500 g (1 lb) cooking
apples, peeled,
cored and sliced*
1 tablespoon water
25 g (1 oz) butter
2 teaspoons sugar

Put the apples and water in a pan,
cover and simmer until tender; drain.
Cool slightly, pour into the blender
and add the butter and sugar. Blend
on maximum speed for 30 seconds.
Makes 350 ml (12 fl oz)

Mint Sauce

*25 g (1 oz) mint,
stalks removed*
*1 tablespoon caster
sugar*
*90 ml (3 fl oz)
vinegar*

Place all ingredients in the blender
and blend on maximum speed for
15 seconds. If necessary, stop the
blender and scrape the leaves onto
the blades.
Makes 120 ml (4 fl oz)

Bread Sauce

*½ small onion,
chopped*
*300 ml (½ pint)
milk*
2 cloves
1 bay leaf
*75 g (3 oz) white
breadcrumbs**
25 g (1 oz) butter
salt and pepper

Place the onion and milk in the
blender and blend on maximum
speed for 30 seconds. Pour into a pan
and add the cloves and bay leaf.
Bring to the boil, then cover and
leave in a warm place for 30 minutes.

Remove the cloves and bay leaf,
stir in the breadcrumbs and beat in
the butter, salt and pepper to taste.
Makes 300 ml (½ pint)

Pesto Sauce

25 g (1 oz) basil,
  stalks removed
25 g (1 oz) parsley,
  stalks removed
1 clove garlic, chopped
25 g (1 oz) pine nuts
  or walnuts
25 g (1 oz) grated
  Parmesan cheese
60 ml (2 fl oz) olive
  oil
salt and pepper

Place all the ingredients in the blender, with salt and pepper to taste. Blend on maximum speed for 30 to 40 seconds.

This Italian sauce is delicious with spaghetti, or use a spoonful in minestrone soup for extra flavour.

Makes 175 ml (6 fl oz)

NOTE: To store pesto, pour it into a screw-topped jar and cover the surface with a thin layer of olive oil. Keep in the refrigerator.

Hollandaise Sauce

3 tablespoons wine
  vinegar
6 black peppercorns
1 small bay leaf
1 mace blade
2 egg yolks
salt
125 g (4 oz) butter,
  melted

Place the vinegar, peppercorns, bay leaf and mace in a small pan and simmer until reduced to 2 teaspoons. Strain into the blender and add the egg yolks, and salt to taste.

Turn the blender on at minimum speed and gradually pour in the butter until the sauce has emulsified. Reheat in a bowl over a pan of simmering water.

Serve warm, with fish and vegetables.

Makes 150 ml (¼ pint)

French Dressing

300 ml (½ pint)
  olive oil
90 ml (3 fl oz) wine
  vinegar
1 teaspoon French
  mustard
1 clove garlic, chopped
2 teaspoons caster
  sugar
salt and pepper

Place all the ingredients in the
blender with salt and pepper to taste.
Blend on maximum speed for
15 seconds. Store in a bottle until
required.

Makes 450 ml (¾ pint)

VARIATION:

Vinaigrette Dressing: Add
2 thyme sprigs, 4 parsley sprigs,
1 mint sprig (all stalks removed) and
a few chives, before blending.

Yogurt Dressing

150 g (5 oz) natural
  low-fat yogurt
2 tablespoons wine
  vinegar
90 ml (3 fl oz) corn
  oil
1 clove garlic, chopped
salt and pepper
1 teaspoon sugar

Place all the ingredients in the
blender and blend on maximum
speed for 15 seconds.
  Serve with salads or fish dishes.

Makes 300 ml (½ pint)

VARIATION:

Herb Dressing: Add 4 parsley
sprigs, 4 mint sprigs, 4 marjoram
sprigs (all stalks removed) and a few
chives, before blending.

Cucumber Dressing

½ cucumber
2 fennel sprigs
2 parsley sprigs
142 ml (5 fl oz)
soured cream
salt and pepper to
taste

Peel the cucumber and chop roughly. Remove stalks from the fennel and parsley. Place all the ingredients in the blender and blend on maximum speed for 1 minute.

Serve with salads or fish dishes.

Makes 300 ml (½ pint)

Mayonnaise

1 egg
½ teaspoon each
salt, pepper and
dry mustard
1 tablespoon wine
vinegar
300 ml (½ pint)
corn oil

Using the Blender: Break in the egg and add the seasonings and vinegar. Blend on medium speed, gradually adding the oil through the lid.

Using the Mixer: Use 2 egg yolks instead of 1 egg. Whisk the yolks and seasonings at medium speed until beginning to thicken. Increase to high speed and slowly pour in a quarter of the oil. Add the vinegar then the remaining oil, a little more quickly.

Makes 300 ml (½ pint)

VARIATION:

Tartare Sauce: Add 1 tablespoon chopped capers, 2 chopped gherkins, 1 teaspoon each chopped chives and parsley to the finished mayonnaise.

Herb and Avocado Dip

1 avocado
114 ml (4 fl oz)
    single cream
4 parsley sprigs,
    stalks removed
few chives
1 clove garlic,
    chopped
1 teaspoon lemon
    juice
salt and pepper

Peel the avocado, halve and remove the stone. Cut the avocado into chunks and place in the blender with the remaining ingredients, adding salt and pepper to taste. Blend on maximum speed for 30 seconds. If necessary, switch off the blender and scrape the mixture back onto the blades.

Spoon into a bowl and serve with savoury biscuits.
Makes 250 ml (8 fl oz)

Stilton Dip

50 g (2 oz) Stilton
    cheese, chopped
113 g (4 oz) cream
    cheese
1 tablespoon port
2 tablespoons milk
2 parsley sprigs,
    stalks removed

Place all the ingredients in the blender and blend on medium speed until smooth. If necessary, switch off the blender and scrape the cheese back onto the blades.

Spoon into a small bowl. Serve with savoury biscuits, or crisp, raw vegetables cut into thin strips.
Makes 250 ml (8 fl oz)

Cream Cheese and Pepper Dip

175 g (6 oz) packet
    cream cheese
3 tablespoons soured
    cream
50 g (2 oz) Cheddar
    cheese, finely
    grated
few drops of Tabasco
    sauce
1 clove garlic,
    crushed
1 small green pepper,
    cored, seeded and
    finely chopped
salt and pepper

Place all the ingredients, except the green pepper, in the mixer bowl, seasoning with salt and pepper to taste. Mix on medium speed until evenly blended.

Turn into a small bowl and stir in the chopped pepper. Cover and chill in the refrigerator for 2 hours.

Spoon into a small bowl. Serve with crisp, raw vegetables, cut into thin strips.
Makes 450 ml (3/4 pint)

MAIN COURSE DISHES

Gougère

2 tablespoons oil
1 onion, chopped
125 g (4 oz)
   mushrooms, sliced
1 tablespoon plain
   flour
150 ml (¼ pint)
   chicken stock
175 g (6 oz) cooked
   chicken, diced
salt and pepper
50 g (2 oz) Cheddar
   cheese, grated
2-egg quantity Choux
   pastry (see page 8)
1 tablespoon fresh
   breadcrumbs*
1 tablespoon chopped
   parsley to garnish

Heat the oil in a pan, add the onion and cook gently for 4 minutes. Add the mushrooms and cook for 2 minutes. Stir in the flour, then add the stock and cook for 2 minutes. Add the chicken and salt and pepper to taste. Keep on one side.

Add the cheese to the prepared choux pastry and beat at high speed for 15 seconds.

Spoon the pastry around the bottom edge of a greased 1.2 litre (2 pint) ovenproof dish, pour the filling into the centre and sprinkle with the breadcrumbs. Bake in a preheated hot oven, 200°C (400°F), Gas Mark 6, for 40 to 45 minutes. Sprinkle with the parsley and serve immediately.
Serves 4

Tuna Fish Balls

500 g (1 lb)
  potatoes, boiled
25 g (1 oz) butter or
  margarine
1 x 198 g (7 oz) can
  tuna fish, drained
  and flaked
2 eggs
2 tablespoons
  chopped parsley
salt and pepper
50 g (2 oz) dried
  breadcrumbs
oil for deep-frying
TO SERVE:
parsley sprigs
lemon wedges
Tartare sauce (see
  page 33)

Drain the potatoes and mash well
with the butter or margarine. Place
in the mixer bowl with the tuna, 1
egg, the parsley, and salt and pepper
to taste. Mix on medium speed until
thoroughly blended.

Turn the mixture onto a floured
surface and shape into 12 balls. Beat
the remaining egg with a pinch of
salt. Dip the fish balls in the egg then
in the breadcrumbs.

Heat the oil and deep-fry the fish
balls until crisp and golden. Drain
well, transfer to a serving bowl and
garnish with parsley. Serve with
lemon wedges and tartare sauce.
Serves 4

Savoury Soufflé Omelet

4 eggs, separated
2 tablespoons milk
salt and pepper
1 tablespoon oil for
  frying
FILLING:
1 tablespoon oil
1 small onion,
  chopped
50 g (2 oz)
  mushrooms, sliced
50 g (2 oz) ham,
  shredded
1 tablespoon chopped
  parsley
2 tablespoons double
  cream
salt and pepper

First make the filling. Heat the oil in a small pan, add the onion and cook until transparent. Add the mushrooms and cook for 1 minute. Add the remaining ingredients, with salt and pepper to taste, and heat gently while making the omelet.

Mix the egg yolks, milk, and salt and pepper to taste in a bowl. Whisk the egg whites on highest speed until stiff, then fold in the yolk mixture.

Heat the oil in a 23 cm (9 inch) omelet pan, pour in the soufflé mixture and spread evenly. Cook over a moderate heat for 1 minute until golden brown underneath.

Put the pan in a preheated moderately hot oven, 200°C (400°F), Gas Mark 6, for 3 minutes, or under a hot grill, until the top is set.

Loosen from the edges of the pan and mark a line across the centre to ease folding. Spread the filling over one half and fold the other half over the top. Serve immediately.
Serves 2

Cheese and Chive Soufflé

25 g (1 oz) butter
25 g (1 oz) plain
  flour
150 ml (¼ pint)
  milk
3 egg yolks
50 g (2 oz) Gruyère
  cheese, grated
25 g (1 oz) Cheddar
  cheese, grated
1 tablespoon chopped
  chives
1 tablespoon chopped
  parsley
salt
cayenne pepper
4 egg whites
TO GARNISH:
paprika
chopped chives

Place the butter, flour and milk in the blender and blend on maximum speed for 20 seconds. Transfer to a saucepan and bring to the boil, stirring constantly, then simmer for 1 minute.

Pour into the mixer bowl and add the egg yolks, cheeses, chives, parsley and salt and cayenne pepper to taste. Mix on medium speed until blended.

Whisk the egg whites on highest speed until stiff, then fold 1 tablespoon into the blended mixture to soften. Gently fold in the remaining whites with a metal spoon.

Turn into an oiled 1.2 litre (2 pint) soufflé dish and cook in a preheated moderately hot oven, 190°C (375°F), Gas Mark 5, for 25 to 30 minutes.

Sprinkle with paprika and chives. Serve immediately.

Serves 4

Toad in the Hole

1 tablespoon oil
500 g (1 lb) pork
    sausages
BATTER:
150 ml (¼ pint)
    milk
150 ml (¼ pint)
    water
1 egg
125 g (4 oz) plain
    flour
pinch of salt

Place the oil in a shallow ovenproof dish, about 20 x 30 cm (8 x 12 inches), and arrange the sausages in it. Cook in a preheated hot oven, 220°C (425°F), Gas Mark 7, for 10 minutes.

Meanwhile, place the batter ingredients in the blender and blend on maximum speed for 30 seconds.

Lower the oven temperature to 200°C (400°F), Gas Mark 6. Pour the batter over the sausages and cook for 25 to 30 minutes, until well risen and golden brown. Serve immediately.
Serves 4

Pork and Mushroom Loaf

MEAT LOAF:
500 g (1 lb) minced
    pork
50 g (2 oz)
    wheatmeal
    breadcrumbs*
1 onion, chopped
50 g (2 oz)
    mushrooms,
    chopped
1 clove garlic, crushed
2 tablespoons
    chopped parsley
2 tablespoons soy
    sauce
90 ml (3 fl oz)
    tomato juice
1 egg
salt and pepper
MUSHROOM SAUCE:
2 tablespoons oil
4 spring onions,
    chopped
75 g (3 oz)
    mushrooms, sliced
1 teaspoon soy sauce
90 ml (3 fl oz)
    soured cream

Place the loaf ingredients, with salt and pepper to taste, in the mixer bowl and mix on medium speed until blended.

Spoon into a 500 g (1 lb) loaf tin and press down well with the back of a spoon. Cover with foil and cook in a preheated moderate oven, 180°C (350°F), Gas Mark 4, for 1¼ to 1½ hours.

To make the sauce, heat the oil in a pan, add the spring onions and mushrooms and cook for 3 minutes, stirring. Add the soy sauce and cream and heat gently.

Pour off the juices from the cooked loaf and turn onto a warmed serving dish. Spoon most of the mushrooms and onions from the sauce over the loaf, using a slotted spoon. Pour the remaining sauce round the loaf. Serve immediately.
Serves 4

Prawn and Tomato Flan

CHEESE PASTRY:
175 g (6 oz) plain
    flour
pinch of salt
½ teaspoon dry
    mustard
pinch of cayenne
75 g (3 oz) butter or
    margarine
50 g (2 oz) Cheddar
    cheese, grated
2 tablespoons water
FILLING:
2 tablespoons oil
1 onion, chopped
150 ml (¼ pint)
    double cream
2 eggs
salt and pepper
175 g (6 oz) prawns
1 tablespoon chopped
    parsley
3 tomatoes, skinned
    and chopped
50 g (2 oz) Cheddar
    cheese, grated

Make the pastry as described on page 8. Roll out and use to line a 20 cm (8 inch) round, or a 15 x 20 cm (6 x 8 inch) rectangular flan dish. Cover with cling film and chill in the refrigerator for 15 minutes.

To make the filling, heat the oil in a pan, add the onion and cook for 4 to 5 minutes until transparent.

Mix together the cream, eggs, and salt and pepper to taste, then stir in the prawns, parsley, tomatoes and onion. Pour into the flan case, sprinkle with the cheese and bake in a moderately hot oven, 200°C (400°F), Gas Mark 6, for 35 to 40 minutes. Serve hot or cold, garnished with whole prawns and parsley sprigs if serving for a special occasion.

Serves 4

NOTE: Use fresh, shelled or frozen prawns. If using frozen ones, defrost and drain thoroughly before use.

Beef and Mushroom Pie

3 tablespoons oil
500 g (1 lb) stewing
  beef, cubed
1 large onion,
  chopped
1 tablespoon
  wholemeal flour
300 ml (½ pint)
  beer
salt and pepper
75 g (6 oz)
  mushrooms,
  quartered
2 tablespoons
  chopped parsley
250 g (8 oz)
  Shortcrust pastry
  (see page 8)
beaten egg to glaze

Heat the oil in a large pan, add the meat and fry quickly until browned all over. Remove the meat and set aside. Add the onion to the pan and fry for 5 minutes until softened. Stir in the flour then add the beer, and salt and pepper to taste. Bring to the boil, stirring. Add the meat, cover and simmer for 2 hours.

Stir in the mushrooms and parsley. Turn into a 900 ml (1½ pint) pie dish.

Roll out the pastry to about 5 cm (2 inches) larger than the pie dish. Cut off a narrow strip all round and place on the dampened edge of the dish; moisten the strip with water. Cover the dish with the pastry, pressing the edges down firmly.

Trim and flute the edges, decorate with pastry leaves and make a hole in the centre. Brush with egg and bake in a preheated moderately hot oven, 200°C (400°F), Gas Mark 6, for 30 minutes. Serve hot.
Serves 4

Hamburgers

750 g (1½ lb)
  minced beef
1 onion, chopped
2 tablespoons
  chopped parsley
1 tablespoon soy
  sauce
1 tablespoon Worcester-
  shire sauce
salt and pepper
oil for shallow-frying
TO SERVE:
4 sesame seed baps
onion rings
tomato slices

Place all the ingredients, with salt and pepper to taste, in the mixer bowl and mix on medium speed until blended.

Divide the mixture into 4 equal portions and, with dampened hands, shape into thick, flat rounds.

Heat the oil in a pan and fry the hamburgers for 5 minutes on each side.

Serve hot, in a bap, between onion rings and tomato slices.

Makes 4 hamburgers

Meatballs in Tomato Sauce

75 g (3 oz) wheat-
  meal bread, cubed
4 parsley sprigs
1 onion, chopped
1 clove garlic, crushed
500 g (1 lb) minced
  pork
1 egg
2 tablespoons water
salt and pepper
4 tablespoons oil for
  shallow-frying
TOMATO SAUCE:
500 g (1 lb)
  tomatoes, skinned
  and chopped
1 clove garlic, chopped
2 parsley sprigs
1 teaspoon sugar
1 tablespoon tomato
  purée
1 teaspoon Worcester-
  shire sauce
TO FINISH:
142 ml (5 fl oz)
  soured cream
1 tablespoon chopped
  parsley

Feed the bread and parsley into the blender through the hole in the lid and blend on maximum speed for 20 seconds. Place in the mixer bowl with the onion, garlic, pork, egg, water, and salt and pepper to taste. Mix on medium speed until well blended. Using dampened hands, shape the mixture into small balls.

Heat the oil in a frying pan, add the meat balls, in batches, and fry until browned, shaking the pan frequently. Drain and place in a 1.2 litre (2 pint) ovenproof dish.

Place all the sauce ingredients, with salt and pepper to taste, in the blender and blend on maximum speed for 15 seconds. Pour over the meatballs and cook in a preheated moderate oven, 180°C (350°F), Gas Mark 4, for 40 minutes.

Spoon over the soured cream and sprinkle with parsley to serve.

Serves 4

Crown Roast of Lamb

To prepare a crown of lamb, remove the chine bones from 2 best ends of neck. Cut through the flesh 2.5 cm (1 inch) from the tip of each bone and scrape these tips clean. Sew the joints together back to back, with the bones curving outwards, using a trussing needle and fine string.

1 crown of lamb
2 tablespoons oil
STUFFING:
4 slices white bread, crusts removed, cubed
4 parsley sprigs
1 rosemary sprig
1 onion, chopped
2 rashers bacon, derinded and diced
3 tablespoons oil
75 g (3 oz) dried apricots, soaked overnight and chopped
salt and pepper to taste
1 egg, beaten

For the stuffing, feed the bread and herbs into the blender through the lid; blend on maximum speed for 20 seconds.

Sauté the onion and bacon in the oil for 5 minutes. Off the heat, stir in the breadcrumb mixture, apricots, salt and pepper, then the egg.

Spoon into the centre of the crown and place in a roasting pan with the oil. Cover the tips of the bones with foil. Cook in a preheated moderately hot oven, 190°C (375°F), Gas Mark 5, allowing 20 minutes per 500 g (1 lb) plus 20 minutes. Baste once or twice during cooking.

Replace the foil with cutlet frills. Transfer to a warmed serving dish and surround with vegetables.
Serves 8

Steak Stuffed with Mushrooms

50 g (2 oz) wheat-
    meal bread, cubed
4 parsley sprigs
1 thyme sprig
2 tablespoons olive
    oil
1 small onion, chopped
1 clove garlic, crushed
3 rashers streaky
    bacon, derinded
    and chopped
50 g (2 oz)
    mushrooms,
    chopped
1 egg yolk
salt and pepper
750 g (1 ½ lb) rump
    steak, cut 3.5 cm
    (1 ½ inches) thick
oil for brushing
2 tablespoons brandy
90 ml (3 fl oz)
    double cream
watercress sprigs to
    garnish

Feed the bread, parsley and thyme into the blender through the lid and blend on maximum speed for 20 seconds.

Heat the oil in a small pan, add the onion and fry for 3 minutes until transparent. Add the garlic, bacon and mushrooms and cook for 5 minutes. Stir in the breadcrumb mixture, egg yolk, and salt and pepper to taste. Cool.

Slit the steak on one side to form a pocket, fill with the stuffing and sew up with a trussing needle and string.

Heat the oil in a heavy frying pan and fry the steak for 5 to 10 minutes on each side, according to taste. Remove the string and transfer to a warmed serving dish.

Add the brandy to the pan, then stir in the cream and heat gently. Pour the sauce around the meat. Cut into thick slices, garnish with watercress and serve immediately.
Serves 4

Prawn and Mushroom Crêpes

BATTER:

125 g (4 oz) plain
  flour
1 egg
300 ml (½ pint)
  milk
1 tablespoon oil
pinch of salt

FILLING:

50 g (2 oz) butter
½ onion, chopped
125 g (4 oz) button
  mushrooms, sliced
2 tablespoons flour
150 ml (¼ pint)
  single cream
150 ml (¼ pint)
  milk
250 g (8 oz) peeled
  prawns
1 tablespoon each
  chopped parsley
  and fennel
salt and pepper
1 tablespoon grated
  Parmesan cheese

Place the batter ingredients in the
blender and blend on maximum
speed for 30 seconds.

Heat a 15 cm (6 inch) omelet pan
and add a few drops of oil. Pour in
1 tablespoon of the batter and tilt the
pan to coat the bottom evenly. Cook
until the underside is brown, then
turn and cook for 10 seconds. Repeat
with the remaining batter, stacking
the pancakes as they are cooked.

To make the filling: melt half the
butter in a pan, add the onion and
cook for 3 minutes. Add the
mushrooms and cook for 2 minutes,
then stir in the flour. Gradually stir
in the cream and milk and cook,
stirring until thickened. Mix in the
prawns, parsley, fennel, and salt and
pepper to taste.

Divide the filling between the
pancakes, roll up and place in a
shallow ovenproof dish. Dot with
the remaining butter and sprinkle
with the cheese. Cook in a preheated
moderately hot oven, 190°C (375°F),
Gas Mark 5, for 15 minutes.
Serves 4

Pizza Napolitana

PIZZA DOUGH:
250 g (8 oz) plain
  flour
½ teaspoon salt
7 g (¼ oz) fresh
  yeast
150 ml (¼ pint)
  warm water
1 tablespoon olive oil
TOPPING:
1 tablespoon tomato
  purée
500 g (1 lb)
  tomatoes, skinned
  and sliced
1 teaspoon chopped
  basil
salt and pepper
250 g (8 oz)
  Mozzarella
  cheese, thinly
  sliced
1 x 49 g (1¾ oz)
  can anchovy
  fillets, halved
  lengthways
½ teaspoon dried
  oregano

Sift the flour and salt together into
the mixer bowl. Cream the yeast
with a little of the water and leave
until frothy. Add to the flour with
the remaining water and the oil.
Using the dough hook, mix and then
knead for 3 minutes on speed 2, until
the dough is smooth and leaves the
sides of the bowl clean.

Cover with a damp cloth and leave
to rise in a warm place for about
1½ hours, until doubled in size.

Knead for 1 minute on speed 2,
then divide the dough in half and
shape each piece into a 20 cm (8 inch)
round. Place on greased baking sheets.

Spread the pizzas with the tomato
purée and arrange the tomatoes on
top. Sprinkle with the basil, and salt
and pepper to taste. Cover with the
cheese and arrange the anchovies in a
lattice pattern over the top. Sprinkle
with the oregano.

Bake in a preheated moderately
hot oven, 200°C (400°F), Gas Mark
6, for 15 to 20 minutes. Serve
immediately.
Serves 4

DESERTS

Zabaione with Macaroons

4 macaroons
4 egg yolks
75 g (3 oz) caster
  sugar
4 tablespoons
  Marsala

Break the macaroons into small pieces and divide equally between 4 glasses.

Place the egg yolks in a bowl with the sugar and Marsala. Whisk together on high speed over a pan of gently simmering water until thick and mousse-like.

Pour over the macaroons and serve immediately, while the zabaione is still warm.

Serves 4

Orange Syllabub

grated rind and juice
  of 2 oranges
grated rind and juice
  of 1 lemon
75 g (3 oz) caster
  sugar
2 tablespoons
  Cointreau
284 ml (10 fl oz)
  double cream

Place the orange and lemon rinds in a bowl with the juices and sugar. Add the Cointreau and leave to soak for 1 hour.

Add the orange mixture to the cream and whisk on medium speed until it holds its shape. Pour into glasses and chill until required. Serve with crisp biscuits.

Serves 6

Apple Tansy

500 g (1 lb) cooking
    apples, peeled,
    cored and sliced
1 tablespoon water
25 g (1 oz) butter
2 eggs, separated
grated rind and juice
    of 1 lemon
75 g (3 oz) caster
    sugar
150 ml (¼ pint)
    double cream,
    whipped
lemon slices to
    decorate

Place the apples in a pan with the
water and butter. Cover and simmer
until the apples are soft. Stir in the
egg yolks. Transfer to the blender,
add the lemon rind and juice and
blend on maximum speed for
30 seconds.

Whisk the egg whites on highest
speed until stiff, then gradually
whisk in the sugar. Fold in the apple
mixture and the cream and spoon
into glasses. Chill until required.
Decorate with lemon slices and serve
with crisp biscuits.
Serves 4 to 6

Strawberry Fool

350 g (12 oz)
    strawberries
50 g (2 oz) caster
    sugar
284 ml (10 fl oz)
    double cream,
    lightly whipped

Set aside 3 strawberries for
decoration. Place the rest in the
blender with the sugar and blend on
maximum speed for 30 seconds.
Sieve to remove pips.

Fold the cream into the strawberry
purée. Spoon into glasses and chill.
Decorate with strawberry halves.
Serves 6

Raspberry Cream

500 g (1 lb)
    raspberries
150 ml (¼ pint)
    water
125 g (4 oz) sugar
15 g (½ oz)
    gelatine, soaked in
    3 tablespoons cold
    water
284 ml (10 fl oz)
    double cream,
    lightly whipped

Set aside 5 of the raspberries for
decoration. Place the rest in the
blender with the water and sugar.
Blend on maximum speed for
15 seconds. Sieve to remove pips.

Heat the gelatine gently until
dissolved, then stir into the raspberry
purée. When just beginning to set,
fold in three quarters of the cream.
Turn into an oiled 1.2 litre (2 pint)
mould and chill until set.

Whip the remaining cream until
thick enough to pipe. Turn out the
raspberry cream and decorate with
piped cream and raspberries.
Serves 6

Pineapple Water Ice

1 large pineapple,
  halved lengthwise
175 g (6 oz)
  granulated sugar
450 ml (¾ pint)
  water
1 egg white

Remove the core from the pineapple. Scrape out the flesh and juice; place in the blender. Blend on maximum speed for 30 seconds. Chill the shells.

Place the sugar and water in a pan and heat gently until dissolved. Boil for 5 minutes, then cool. Add the pineapple pulp and pour into a rigid freezerproof container. Cover, seal and freeze for 3 hours, until half-frozen.

Whisk the egg white on highest speed until stiff, then gradually whisk in the water ice, on medium speed, until frothy. Cover, seal and freeze until firm.

Transfer to the refrigerator 10 minutes before serving. Scoop into the pineapple shells to serve.
Serves 6 to 8

Apple and Calvados Sorbet

750 g (1½ lb)
  cooking apples,
  peeled, cored and
  sliced
450 ml (¾ pint)
  water
grated rind and juice
  of 1 lemon
175 g (6 oz) sugar
1 egg white
1-2 tablespoons
  Calvados
mint leaves to
  decorate

Place the apples in a pan with 150 ml (¼ pint) of the water. Cover and simmer until soft. Cool slightly, pour into the blender and add the lemon rind and juice. Blend on maximum speed for 30 seconds. Cool completely.

Heat the remaining water with the sugar, gently until dissolved. Boil for 5 minutes then cool. Add the apple purée, then pour into a rigid freezer-proof container. Cover, seal and freeze for 3 hours, until half-frozen.

Whisk the egg white on highest speed until stiff, then gradually whisk in the water ice, on medium speed, until frothy. Cover, seal and freeze for 2 hours.

Whisk in the Calvados. Cover, seal and re-freeze until firm.

Transfer to the refrigerator 10 minutes before serving. Decorate with mint leaves.
Serves 6 to 8

Apricot Ice Cream

350 g (12 oz) dried
  apricots, soaked in
  water for 2 hours
2 tablespoons lemon
  juice
3 egg whites
175 g (6 oz) caster
  sugar
284 ml (10 fl oz)
  double cream, or
  imitation cream,
  whipped

Place the apricots and soaking liquid in a pan, adding enough water to cover. Simmer gently, covered, for 20 minutes. Drain, reserving 150 ml (¼ pint) liquid. Cool slightly, then put the apricots, reserved liquid and lemon juice into the blender and blend on maximum speed for 30 seconds. Cool completely.

Whisk the egg whites on highest speed until stiff, then gradually whisk in the sugar. Fold the cream and apricot purée into the meringue mixture. Turn into a rigid freezerproof container. Cover, seal and freeze until solid.

Transfer to the refrigerator 30 minutes before serving to soften.
Serves 6 to 8

Blackcurrant Freezies

350 g (12 oz)
  blackcurrants,
  stalks removed
175 g (6 oz) caster
  sugar
2 teaspoons gelatine,
  soaked in 2
  tablespoons water
500 ml (18 fl oz)
  orange cream (see
  page 63), or
  imitation cream,
  stiffly whipped
2 egg whites
blackcurrant leaves to
  decorate

Place the blackcurrants in a pan with 75 g (3 oz) of the sugar. Cover and simmer gently for 15 minutes.

Cool slightly, then pour into the blender and blend on maximum speed for 30 seconds. Turn into a bowl to cool.

Heat the gelatine gently until dissolved, then fold into the blackcurrant purée. Carefully fold in the orange cream.

Whisk the egg whites on high speed until stiff, then gradually whisk in the remaining sugar. Fold into the blackcurrant mixture. Turn into 8 ramekins and freeze for 2 to 3 hours. Decorate with blackcurrant leaves before serving.
Serves 8

Bramble Mousse

350 g (12 oz)
   blackberries
1 tablespoon water
2 eggs
1 egg yolk
75 g (3 oz) caster
   sugar
15 g (½ oz)
   gelatine, soaked in
   3 tablespoons cold
   water
284 ml (10 fl oz)
   double cream, or
   imitation cream,
   lightly whipped

Set aside a few blackberries. Place the rest in a pan with the water and simmer gently for 5 minutes. Cool slightly, then pour into the blender. Blend on maximum speed for 30 seconds. Sieve to remove pips.

Place the eggs, egg yolk and sugar in the mixer bowl and whisk on high speed for 5 minutes until thick.

Heat the gelatine gently until dissolved, then fold into the egg mousse with the blackberry purée and half the cream.

Turn into a 1.2 litre (2 pint) glass dish and chill until set. Whip the remaining cream at medium speed until stiff. Decorate the mousse with piped cream and blackberries.
Serves 6 to 8

Apple Fritters

50 g (2 oz) plain
  flour
1 egg, separated
4 tablespoons water
1 teaspoon oil
2 large cooking
  apples, peeled and
  cored
oil for deep-frying
icing sugar for
  dredging

Place the flour, egg yolk, water and
oil in the blender and blend on
maximum speed for 30 seconds.
Pour into a bowl.

Cut the apples into 5 mm (¼ inch)
rings. Whisk the egg white on
highest speed and fold into the batter.

Dip the apples in the batter,
draining off any excess, then deep-
fry in hot oil for 2 to 3 minutes until
golden.

Drain on kitchen paper, dredge
with icing sugar and serve with
cream.

Serves 4

Apple and Orange Flan

175 g (6 oz) rich
  shortcrust pastry
  (see page 8)
1 kg (2 lb) cooking
  apples, peeled and
  cored
1 tablespoon water
50 g (2 oz) caster
  sugar
3 oranges
GLAZE:
4 tablespoons apricot
  jam
2 tablespoons water
1 teaspoon lemon
  juice
TO SERVE:
whipped cream

Roll out the pastry and use to line a
20 cm (8 inch) flan ring standing on a
baking sheet. Line with greaseproof
paper and dried beans and bake in a
preheated moderately hot oven,
200°C (400°F), Gas Mark 6, for 15 to
20 minutes. Remove the paper and
beans and return to the oven for 5
minutes. Remove the flan ring and
cool on a wire rack.

Slice the apples and place in a pan
with the water and sugar. Cover and
cook gently to a pulp, stirring
occasionally. Cool slightly, then
pour into the blender and blend on
maximum speed for 30 seconds.
Return to the pan and add the grated
rind of 2 oranges. Cook, uncovered,
until thick, stirring occasionally.
Leave until cool, then turn into the
flan case and smooth evenly.

Peel the oranges, removing all
pith. Slice thinly and arrange on top
of the flan. Heat the jam with the
water and lemon juice, then sieve
and reheat. Brush over the oranges.
Serve with whipped cream.

Serves 6

Caramel Vacherin

4 egg whites
250 g (8 oz) soft
  brown sugar
50 g (2 oz)
  hazelnuts,
  browned and
  chopped
284 ml (10 fl oz)
  double cream
8 hazelnuts to
  decorate

Whisk the egg whites on highest speed until stiff and dry looking. Gradually whisk in the sugar. Put the meringue into a piping bag, fitted with a 1 cm (½ inch) plain nozzle. Pipe two 23 cm (9 inch) rounds on baking sheets lined with silicone paper. Sprinkle a few of the chopped nuts over one round.

Bake in a very cool oven, 120°C (250°F), Gas Mark ½, for 2 hours until crisp. Peel off the paper and cool the meringue rounds on a wire rack.

Whip the cream until it holds its shape. Combine three quarters of the cream with the remaining chopped nuts and use to sandwich the meringues together, with the nutty round on top. Pipe the remaining cream around the edge and decorate with the hazelnuts.

Serves 6 to 8

Strawberry Cheesecake

125 g (4 oz)
  digestive biscuits
25 g (1 oz) demerara
  sugar
50 g (2 oz) butter or
  margarine, melted
340 g (12 oz)
  cottage cheese
50 g (2 oz) caster
  sugar
grated rind and juice
  of 1 lemon
2 eggs, separated
284 ml (10 fl oz)
  single cream
15 g (½ oz) gelatine
TO FINISH:
125 g (4 oz)
  strawberries
114 ml (4 fl oz)
  double cream,
  whipped

Break the biscuits into pieces and place in the blender. Blend on maximum speed for 20 seconds. Combine the crumbs, demerara sugar and butter. Spread the mixture over the base of a 20 cm (8 inch) loose-bottomed cake tin and chill until firm.

Place the cheese in the blender with the caster sugar, lemon rind and juice, egg yolks and cream. Soak the gelatine in 3 tablespoons cold water, then heat gently until dissolved. Pour into the blender and blend on maximum speed for 30 seconds. Turn into a bowl.

Whisk the egg whites on highest speed until stiff then fold into the cheese mixture. Spoon over the biscuit base and chill until set.

Transfer to a serving dish, arrange the strawberries on top and pipe the cream around the edge.
Serves 8

Crêpes aux Bananas

BATTER:
125 g (4 oz) plain
   flour
pinch of salt
1 tablespoon icing
   sugar
1 tablespoon instant
   coffee powder
300 ml (½ pint)
   milk
1 tablespoon oil
1 egg
FILLING:
6 bananas
25 g (1 oz) butter,
   melted
2 tablespoons brandy
TO SERVE:
2 tablespoons flaked
   almonds, toasted
whipped cream

Place the batter ingredients in the blender and blend on maximum speed for 30 seconds.

Heat a 15 cm (6 inch) omelet pan and add a few drops of oil. Pour in 1 tablespoon batter, tilting the pan to coat the bottom evenly. Cook until the underside is brown, then turn and cook for 10 seconds. Repeat with the remaining batter, stacking the pancakes as they are cooked.

Cut the bananas in half lengthways and wrap each half in a pancake. Place in a shallow ovenproof dish, brush with the butter and pour over the brandy. Bake in a preheated moderate oven, 180°C (350°F), Gas Mark 4, for 15 minutes. Sprinkle with the almonds and serve with cream.
Serves 6

Orange and Rhubarb Pudding

500 g (1 lb) rhubarb
grated rind and juice
   of 1 orange
50 g (2 oz) soft
   brown sugar
PUDDING MIXTURE:
50 g (2 oz) soft
   margarine
50 g (2 oz) soft
   brown sugar
1 large egg
75 g (3 oz) self-
   raising flour, sifted
½ teaspoon baking
   powder
50 g (2 oz) almonds,
   chopped
TO SERVE:
orange cream (see
   opposite)

Cut the rhubarb into 2.5 cm (1 inch) lengths and place in a 900 ml (1½ pint) ovenproof dish. Pour over the orange juice and sprinkle with the orange rind and sugar.

Warm the mixer bowl and beaters. Place all the pudding ingredients, except the almonds, in the bowl and beat on slow speed until combined. Increase to maximum speed and beat for 40 seconds.

Spoon over the rhubarb mixture and spread evenly to the edges. Sprinkle the almonds over the top and bake in a preheated moderate oven, 180°C (350°F), Gas Mark 4, for 35 to 40 minutes. Serve hot, with orange cream.
Serves 4

Orange Cream

This is a good accompaniment to serve with pies and crumbles instead of cream.

250 g (8 oz)
    unsalted butter
300 ml (½ pint)
    milk
1 teaspoon gelatine
grated rind of 1
    orange
1 tablespoon caster
    sugar

Place all the ingredients in a pan and heat very gently until the butter has melted. Cool until lukewarm, then pour into the blender and blend on maximum speed for 30 seconds.

Chill in the refrigerator and whisk lightly before use.

This cream can also be whisked stiffly and used for piping.

Makes 500 ml (18 fl oz)

CAKES, BISCUITS & BREADS

Choux Buns

2-egg quantity
  Choux pastry (see
  page 8)
150 ml (¼ pint)
  double cream,
  whipped
icing sugar

Place spoonfuls of the pastry on a dampened baking sheet and bake in a preheated moderately hot oven, 200°C (400°F), Gas Mark 6, for 25 to 30 minutes until crisp and golden brown. Make a slit in the side of each bun to allow the steam to escape and cool on a wire rack.

Put the cream into a piping bag fitted with a 5 mm (¼ inch) plain nozzle and pipe a little into each bun. Sprinkle with icing sugar to serve.
Makes 10 buns

Meringues

2 egg whites
125 g (4 oz) caster
 sugar
TO FINISH:
114 ml (4 fl oz)
 double cream,
 whipped

Place the egg whites in the mixer bowl and whisk on highest speed until stiff and dry. Add half the sugar and whisk until mixed. Fold in the remaining sugar with a metal spoon.

Put the mixture into a piping bag fitted with a 1 cm (½ inch) plain nozzle and pipe into mounds on a baking sheet lined with oiled greaseproof paper or non-stick parchment.

Bake in a preheated very cool oven, 110°C (225°F), Gas Mark ¼, for 2 to 3 hours until crisp.

Sandwich the meringues together in pairs with the cream to serve.
Makes 8

Date and Apple Scones

250 g (8 oz) plain
  flour
½ teaspoon mixed
  spice
1 teaspoon cream of
  tartar
½ teaspoon
  bicarbonate of soda
50 g (2 oz) butter or
  margarine, cut into
  pieces
25 g (1 oz) soft
  brown sugar
50 g (2 oz) dates,
  chopped
1 small cooking
  apple, peeled,
  cored and grated
3 tablespoons milk
milk to glaze

Sift the flour, spice, cream of tartar and bicarbonate of soda into the mixer bowl. Add the fat and mix on slowest speed until combined. Increase speed slightly and beat until the mixture resembles breadcrumbs. Add the sugar, dates and apple and mix well. Add the milk a little at a time and mix on slow speed to a soft dough.

Turn onto a floured surface, knead lightly and roll out to a 2 cm (¾ inch) thickness. Cut into 5 cm (2 inch) rounds with a fluted cutter. Place on a floured baking sheet and brush with milk. Bake in a preheated hot oven, 220°C (425°F), Gas Mark 7, for 12 to 15 minutes. Transfer to a wire rack to cool.

Makes 12 to 14

VARIATION:

Fruit scones: Omit mixed spice and apple. Replace dates with 75 g (3 oz) currants. Use 5 tablespoons milk.

Nutty Shortbread Fingers

125 g (4 oz) butter
  or soft margarine
50 g (2 oz) caster
  sugar
125 g (4 oz) plain
  flour
50 g (2 oz) ground
  rice
50 g (2 oz) almonds,
  finely chopped

Place the fat and sugar in the mixer bowl and beat on medium speed until light and fluffy. Add the flour, rice and two thirds of the nuts. Mix on medium speed until blended.

Turn onto a lightly floured board and knead until smooth. Roll out to an oblong and press into an 18 x 28 cm (7 x 11 inch) Swiss roll tin. Flatten with a palette knife and prick all over with a fork. Sprinkle over the remaining nuts, pressing in lightly.

Bake in a preheated moderate oven, 160°C (325°F), Gas Mark 3, for 50 to 55 minutes, until pale golden. Leave in the tin for 5 minutes, then mark into 18 fingers. Cool completely before removing from the tin.

Makes 18

Coconut Macaroons

2 egg whites
150 g (5 oz) caster
  sugar
150 g (5 oz)
  desiccated coconut
rice paper
5 glacé cherries,
  quartered

Whisk the egg whites on high speed until just stiff, then whisk in the sugar. Mix in the coconut on medium speed. Place heaped teaspoonfuls of the mixture on a baking sheet lined with rice paper. Top each with a glacé cherry piece.

Bake in a preheated moderate oven, 160°C (325°F), Gas Mark 3, for 30 minutes. Leave on the baking sheet until cold, then tear off the rice paper.
Makes 18 to 20

Refrigerator Biscuits

125 g (4 oz) butter
or margarine
125 g (4 oz) caster
sugar
1 small egg, beaten
1 teaspoon vanilla
essence
250 g (8 oz) plain
flour, sifted

Place the fat and sugar in the mixer bowl. Beat on medium speed until light and fluffy, then beat in the egg and vanilla. Mix in the flour on slow speed to form a soft dough.

Knead on a lightly floured surface until smooth. Shape into a long roll, 3.5 cm (1½ inches) in diameter. Wrap in foil and chill for 1 hour.

Remove foil, cut into 5 mm (¼ inch) thick slices and place slightly apart on a baking sheet. Bake in a preheated moderately hot oven, 200°C (400°F), Gas Mark 6, for 7 to 8 minutes until golden. Leave on the baking tray for 1 minute then transfer to a wire rack to cool.

Makes about 45

VARIATIONS:

Nutty Biscuits: Add 50 g (2 oz) chopped hazelnuts with the flour.
Cherry Biscuits: Add 50 g (2 oz) chopped glacé cherries and 25 g (1 oz) chopped angelica with the flour.
Chocolate Biscuits: Replace 2 tablespoons flour with 2 tablespoons cocoa powder.

Chocolate Cookies

175 g (6 oz) plain
flour
1 teaspoon baking
powder
pinch of bicarbonate
of soda
75 g (3 oz) butter or
margarine
50 g (2 oz) soft
brown sugar
3 tablespoons golden
syrup
50 g (2 oz) plain
cooking chocolate,
chopped

Sift the flour, baking powder and bicarbonate of soda into the mixer bowl. Add the fat and beat on slowest speed, increasing slightly until the mixture resembles breadcrumbs. Mix in the remaining ingredients on slow speed.

Form into balls, about the size of a walnut, and place slightly apart on a greased baking sheet. Press gently to flatten slightly.

Bake in a moderately hot oven, 190°C (375°F), Gas Mark 5, for 15 minutes until golden brown. Transfer to a wire rack to cool.

Makes 24

Victoria Sandwich Cake

125 g (4 oz) butter
  or soft margarine
125 g (4 oz) caster
  sugar
2 eggs
125 g (4 oz)
  self-raising flour,
  sifted
1 tablespoon hot
  water
TO FINISH:
3 tablespoons jam
caster sugar

Warm the mixer bowl and beaters
thoroughly. Place the fat and sugar
in the bowl and mix on medium
speed until combined. Turn to high
speed and beat until light and fluffy,
scraping the mixture from the sides
of the bowl as necessary. Add the
eggs one at a time, adding a tablespoon of the flour with the second
egg; beat thoroughly on high speed.

Fold in the remaining flour with a
metal spoon then fold in the water.
Divide the mixture between 2 lined
and greased 18 cm (7 inch) sandwich
tins, and bake in a preheated
moderate oven, 180°C (350°F), Gas
Mark 4, for 20 to 25 minutes, until
the cakes spring back when lightly
pressed. Turn onto a wire rack to
cool.

Sandwich the cakes together with
the jam and sprinkle with sugar.
Makes one 18 cm (7 inch) cake

Whisked Sponge

2 eggs
75 g (3 oz) caster
   sugar
50 g (2 oz) plain
   flour
TO FINISH:
114 ml (4 fl oz)
   double cream
2 tablespoons
   raspberry jam
icing sugar

Place the eggs and sugar in the mixer bowl and whisk on high speed for 5 to 7 minutes until thick and mousse-like.

Fold in the flour carefully with a metal spoon, then turn into a lined and greased 20 cm (8 inch) sandwich tin. Bake in a preheated moderately hot oven, 190°C (375°F), Gas Mark 5, for 30 to 35 minutes, until the cake springs back when lightly pressed. Turn onto a wire rack to cool.

Split the cake in half, then sandwich together with the cream and jam. Sprinkle with icing sugar.
Makes one 20 cm (8 inch) cake
VARIATIONS:
Chocolate: Replace 1 tablespoon of the flour with cocoa powder.
Coffee: Add 2 teaspoons instant coffee powder or crushed coffee granules with the flour.

71

One-Stage Fruit Cake

*175 g (6 oz) soft
margarine
175 g (6 oz) soft
brown sugar
3 eggs
1 tablespoon black
treacle
125 g (4 oz) glacé
cherries, quartered
125 g (4 oz)
sultanas
125 g (4 oz) raisins
250 g (8 oz)
self-raising flour
1 teaspoon mixed
spice*

Grease a deep 20 cm (8 inch) round
cake tin and line the base and sides
with a double layer of greased
greaseproof paper.

Place all the ingredients in the
mixer bowl and beat on slowest
speed until combined. Increase to
medium speed and beat for
30 seconds. Turn into the prepared
tin and bake in a preheated moderate
oven, 160°C (325°F), Gas Mark 3, for
1½ to 1¾ hours, or until a skewer
inserted into the centre comes out
clean. Leave in the tin for 5 minutes,
then turn onto a wire rack to cool.
Makes one 20 cm (8 inch) cake

One-Stage Sandwich Cake

125 g (4 oz) soft margarine
125 g (4 oz) caster sugar
2 eggs
125 g (4 oz) self-raising flour, sifted
1 teaspoon baking powder, sifted
COFFEE FILLING:
50 g (2 oz) soft margarine
125 g (4 oz) icing sugar, sifted
2 teaspoons coffee essence
25 g (1 oz) hazel-nuts, chopped and toasted
TO FINISH:
icing sugar

Warm the mixer bowl and beaters. Place all the cake ingredients in the bowl and beat on slow speed until combined. Increase to highest speed and beat for 40 seconds.

Divide the mixture between two lined and greased 18 cm (7 inch) sandwich tins. Bake in a preheated moderate oven, 160°C (325°F), Gas Mark 3, for 30 to 35 minutes until the cakes spring back when lightly pressed. Turn onto a wire rack to cool.

To make the filling, place all the ingredients in the mixer bowl and beat on slow speed until combined. Increase to high speed and beat until light and fluffy. Sandwich the cakes together with the filling and sprinkle with icing sugar.

Makes one 18 cm (7 inch) cake

Chocolate Chip Cake

*175 g (6 oz) butter
or soft margarine*
*175 g (6 oz) caster
sugar*
3 eggs
*250 g (8 oz)
self-raising flour*
*125 g (4 oz) plain
cooking chocolate,
chopped*
*50 g (2 oz) ground
almonds*
2 tablespoons milk
*25 g (1 oz) chopped
almonds*

Warm the mixer bowl and beaters. Place the fat and sugar in the bowl and beat on medium speed until combined. Increase to high speed and beat until light and fluffy, scraping the sides of the bowl as necessary. Add the eggs one at a time, adding 1 tablespoon of the flour with the last two, beating on high speed.

Fold in the remaining flour, the chocolate and ground almonds, with a metal spoon, then fold in the milk.

Place the mixture in a lined and greased deep 18 cm (7 inch) cake tin and sprinkle with the chopped almonds. Bake in a preheated moderate oven, 180°C (350°F), Gas Mark 4, for 1½ hours.

Leave in the tin for 5 minutes, then turn onto a wire rack to cool.
Makes one 18 cm (7 inch) cake

Chocolate Sandwich Cake

125 g (4 oz) plain
  flour
2 teaspoons baking
  powder
pinch of bicarbonate
  of soda
50 g (2 oz) cocoa
  powder
120 ml (4 fl oz) corn
  oil
250 g (8 oz) caster
  sugar
120 ml (4 fl oz)
  milk
FILLING:
114 ml (4 fl oz)
  double cream,
  whipped
TOPPING:
50 g (2 oz) plain
  cooking chocolate

Sift the flour, baking powder,
bicarbonate of soda and cocoa
together into the mixer bowl. Add
remaining ingredients and beat on
slow speed until combined. Increase
to medium speed for 30 seconds.

Divide the mixture between two
lined and greased 20 cm (8 inch)
sandwich tins. Bake in a preheated
moderate oven, 180°C (350°F), Gas
Mark 4, for 35 to 40 minutes, until
the cakes spring back when lightly
pressed. Turn onto a wire rack to cool.

Sandwich the cakes together with
all but 1 tablespoon of the whipped
cream. Place the chocolate and
remaining cream in a heatproof bowl
over a pan of hot water and stir until
melted. Cool slightly, then pour over
the cake to coat evenly.

Makes one 20 cm (8 inch) cake

Almond Paste

500 g (1 lb) ground
  almonds
250 g (8 oz) icing
  sugar, sifted
250 g (8 oz) caster
  sugar, sifted
2 small eggs
2 teaspoons lemon
  juice
few drops almond
  essence

Place the almonds and sugars in the mixer bowl and mix together on slowest speed. Add the remaining ingredients and gradually increase the speed until a smooth paste is formed.
Sufficient to cover top and sides of a 23 cm (9 inch) round cake

Royal Icing

3 egg whites
750 g (1½ lb) icing
  sugar, sifted
1 teaspoon lemon
  juice
1½ teaspoons
  glycerine

Beat the egg whites on highest speed for 30 seconds. Turn to slowest speed and gradually add the icing sugar, lemon juice and glycerine.

Turn to medium speed and beat until smooth and stiff enough to form peaks; do not over beat.
Sufficient to cover top and sides of a 23 cm (9 inch) round cake

Butter Icing

125 g (4 oz) butter,
  softened
250 g (8 oz) icing
  sugar, sifted
2 tablespoons milk
flavouring (see
  below)

Warm the mixer bowl and beaters. Beat the butter on medium speed to soften. Add the remaining ingredients and beat on slow speed until incorporated. Turn to medium speed and beat until fluffy.
Sufficient to fill and cover a 20 cm (8 inch) sandwich cake
FLAVOURINGS:
Chocolate: Mix 2 tablespoons cocoa powder with 2 tablespoons boiling water. Cool, then add with the other ingredients, using only 1 tablespoon milk.
Coffee: Replace 1 tablespoon milk with 1 tablespoon coffee essence.
Orange or lemon: Add the grated rind of 1 orange or lemon with the butter. Replace the milk with 2 tablespoons orange or lemon juice.

Crème Patissière

2 eggs, separated
3 tablespoons
  cornflour
300 ml (½ pint) hot
  milk
few drops vanilla
  essence
50 g (2 oz) caster
  sugar

Place the egg yolks, cornflour and milk in the blender and blend on maximum speed for 10 seconds. Pour into a pan, bring to the boil, stirring, and cook, stirring, for 2 minutes. Add the vanilla. Turn into a bowl and cool until lukewarm.

Whisk the egg whites on highest speed until stiff, then gradually whisk in the sugar. Whisk into the cream mixture. Cover with cling film and chill until required.
Makes about 300 ml (½ pint)

Daily Bread

750 g (1½ lb) strong
   white plain flour
2 teaspoons salt
15 g (½ oz) fresh
   yeast
450 ml (¾ pint)
   warm water
1 tablespoon oil
flour for sprinkling

Place the flour and salt in the mixer bowl. Cream the yeast with a little of the water and leave until frothy. Add to the flour with the remaining water and the oil. Using the dough hook, mix and then knead on speed 2 for 3 minutes until the dough is smooth and leaves the sides of the bowl clean.

Cover with a damp cloth and leave to rise in a warm place for about 1½ hours, until doubled in size.

Knead for 1 minute on speed 2. Shape the dough and place in a greased 1 kg (2 lb) loaf tin. Make slits along the top of the loaf. Cover and leave in a warm place for 30 minutes, or until risen to the top of the tin.

Sprinkle with flour and bake in a preheated hot oven, 220°C (425°F), Gas Mark 7, for 15 minutes. Lower the heat to 190°C (375°F), Gas Mark 5, and bake for a further 25 minutes or until the bread sounds hollow when tapped. Cool on a wire rack.
Makes one 1 kg (2 lb) loaf

Light Rye Bread

15 g (½ oz) fresh
  yeast
150 ml (¼ pint)
  warm water
1 tablespoon clear
  honey
250 g (8 oz) rye
  flour
400 g (14 oz) plain
  strong white flour
2 teaspoons salt
300 ml (½ pint)
  warm milk
1 teaspoon caraway
  seeds
egg yolk for glazing

Mix the yeast with the water and honey and leave until frothy. Mix the flours and salt together in the mixer bowl. Add the yeast mixture, milk and half the caraway seeds.

Using the dough hook, mix and then knead on speed 2 for 3 minutes until the dough is smooth and leaves the sides of the bowl clean.

Cover with a damp cloth and leave to rise in a warm place for 1½ to 2 hours until almost doubled in size.

Knead for 1 minute on speed 2. Turn onto a floured surface and shape into a sausage about 25 cm (10 inches) long. Prick with a fork in 8 or 9 places. Cover and leave to rise in a warm place for about 30 minutes.

Brush with egg yolk and sprinkle with remaining caraway seeds. Bake in a moderately hot oven, 200°C (400°F), Gas Mark 6, for 20 minutes. Lower the heat to 190°C (375°F), Gas Mark 5, and bake for a further 15 minutes until the bread sounds hollow when tapped. Cool on a wire rack.
Makes one 750 g (1½ lb) loaf

Quick Brown Bread

1 x 25 mg vitamin C
  tablet
450 ml (³/4 pint)
  warm water
25 g (1 oz) fresh
  yeast
500 g (1 lb)
  wholemeal flour
250 g (8 oz) plain
  strong white flour
2 teaspoons salt
porridge oats for
  sprinkling

Crush the tablet and stir into a little of the water with the yeast. Allow to dissolve, then stir to a cream. Place the flours and salt in the mixer bowl, then add the yeast mixture and remaining water.

Using the dough hook, mix on speed 2 for 3 minutes until the dough is smooth and leaves the sides of the bowl clean. Cover with a damp cloth and leave to rise in a warm place for 15 minutes until doubled in size.

Knead for 1 minute on speed 2 then divide in half, shape and place in two greased 500 g (1 lb) loaf tins. Brush with water and sprinkle with oats.

Cover and leave in a warm place for about 15 minutes until risen to the top of the tins. Bake in a pre-heated hot oven, 220°C (425°F), Gas Mark 7, for 20 minutes. Lower the heat to 190°C (375°F), Gas Mark 5, and bake for a further 15 to 20 minutes until the bread sounds hollow when tapped. Cool on a wire rack.
Makes two 500 g (1 lb) loaves

Granary Rolls

500 g (1 lb) granary
   flour
1 teaspoon salt
15 g (½ oz) fresh
   yeast
300 ml (½ pint)
   warm water
1 tablespoon malt
   extract
1 tablespoon oil
cracked wheat

Put the flour and salt in the mixer
bowl. Cream the yeast with a little of
the water and leave until frothy. Add
to the flour with the malt extract, oil
and remaining water. Using the
dough hook, mix and then knead on
speed 2 for 3 minutes until the dough
is smooth and leaves the sides of the
bowl clean.

Cover with a damp cloth and leave
to rise in a warm place for about
1½ hours, until doubled in size.

Knead for 1 minute on speed 2,
then divide the dough into 14 pieces
and shape into rolls. Place on greased
baking sheets, brush with water and
sprinkle with cracked wheat.

Cover and leave in a warm place for
about 20 minutes until almost doubled
in size. Bake in a preheated hot oven,
220°C (425°F), Gas Mark 7, for 10 to
15 minutes. Cool on a wire rack.
Makes 12

DRINKS & COCKTAILS

Vegetable Cocktail

1 carrot, chopped
1 celery stick,
    chopped
4 parsley sprigs,
    stalks removed
150 ml (¼ pint)
    water
1 teaspoon
    Worcestershire
    sauce
salt and pepper
150 ml (¼ pint)
    tomato juice
chopped chives to
    garnish

Place all the ingredients, except the tomato juice, in the blender, adding salt and pepper to taste. Blend on maximum speed for 30 seconds, then strain.

Mix with the tomato juice, then taste and adjust the seasoning. Pour into glasses and sprinkle with chopped chives to serve.
Serves 2

Tomato Juice

500 g (1 lb) ripe
  tomatoes
1 teaspoon salt
1 teaspoon lemon
  juice
1 teaspoon soft
  brown sugar
1 teaspoon
  Worcestershire
  sauce
300 ml (½ pint)
  water
1 teaspoon tomato
  purée
pepper
TO GARNISH:
4 mint sprigs
4 lemon slices

Skin the tomatoes and chop them roughly. Place all the ingredients, with pepper to taste, in the blender and blend on maximum speed for 30 seconds. Sieve to remove the seeds, then chill.

Pour the tomato juice into glasses and garnish with mint sprigs and lemon slices to serve.

Makes 600 ml (1 pint)

Orange Juice

2 thin-skinned oranges
2-3 tablespoons caster
    sugar
750 ml (1¼ pints)
    cold water
orange slices to
    decorate

Chop the oranges roughly and place
in the blender with the sugar and
water. Blend on maximum speed for
10 seconds.

Strain into glasses and top with
orange slices.

Serves 4 to 5

Caribbean Refresher

juice of 1 orange
juice of 1 lime
2 slices pineapple,
    chopped
1 tablespoon
    Muscovado sugar
2 tablespoons rum
2 ice cubes
150 ml (¼ pint)
    soda water
mint sprigs to decorate

Place all the ingredients, except the
soda water, in the blender and blend
on maximum speed for 30 seconds.

Strain into glasses and top up with
soda water. Decorate with the mint
to serve.

Serves 3

Lemon Froth

juice of 2 lemons
2 tablespoons caster
  sugar
1 egg white
300 ml (½ pint)
  water
2 ice cubes
2 lemon slices to
  decorate

Place all the ingredients in the
blender and blend on maximum
speed for 30 seconds. Pour into
glasses and decorate with lemon
slices to serve.
Serves 2

Honey and Mint Cooler

2 tablespoons clear
  honey
8 mint leaves
juice of 1 lemon
300 ml (½ pint)
  water
4 ice cubes
2 mint sprigs to
  decorate

Place all the ingredients in the
blender. Blend on maximum speed
for 40 seconds.
  Pour into glasses and decorate
with mint sprigs to serve.
Serves 2

Avocado and Strawberry Whizz

75 g (3 oz)
    strawberries
1 small avocado,
    peeled, halved and
    stoned
300 ml (½ pint)
    chilled milk
1 teaspoon lemon
    juice
1 tablespoon caster
    sugar
4 tablespoons single
    cream
lemon balm sprigs

Cut the strawberries in half and set aside 2 pieces for decoration. Cut the avocado into pieces and place in the blender with the strawberries, milk, lemon juice, sugar and cream. Blend on maximum speed for 30 seconds. Strain.

Pour into glasses. Decorate each one with a strawberry slice and a sprig of lemon balm.

Serves 2

Yogurt and Strawberry Whip

125 g (4 oz)
    strawberries
150 ml (¼ pint)
    chilled milk
150 g (5 oz) natural
    low-fat yogurt
juice of ½ orange
1 tablespoon honey
2 scoops vanilla ice
    cream

Reserve one strawberry to decorate.
Place the remainder in the blender
with the milk, yogurt, orange juice
and honey. Blend on maximum
speed for 30 seconds. Strain, pour
into glasses and top each with a
scoop of ice cream. Decorate each
with half a strawberry.

Serves 2

Banana Flip

150 g (5 oz) natural
    low-fat yogurt
150 ml (¼ pint) cold
    milk
1 large banana
1 tablespoon soft
    brown sugar
1 egg

Place all ingredients in the blender.
Blend on maximum speed for 20
seconds until smooth and frothy.
Pour into glasses.

Serves 2

Seychelles Surprise

½ mango
juice of 1 small
  orange
juice of 1 lime
3 tablespoons white
  rum
2 ice cubes
1 egg white, lightly
  beaten
25 g (1 oz) caster
  sugar
150 ml (¼ pint)
  soda water
TO DECORATE:
orange or lime slices,
  or lemon balm
  sprigs

Peel the mango, remove the seeds
and chop the flesh. Place in the
blender with the fruit juices, rum and
ice cubes. Blend on maximum speed
for 30 seconds.

Dip the tops of the glasses into the
egg white, then into the sugar to
give a frosted effect.

Divide the mango mixture
between the glasses and top up with
soda water. Decorate with orange or
lime slices, or lemon balm sprigs.
Serves 4

Banana Fizz

1 banana
1 slice pineapple
juice of ½ lemon
1 tablespoon caster
    sugar
150 ml (¼ pint)
    lemonade
crushed ice to serve

Place all the ingredients, except the lemonade, in the blender. Blend on maximum speed for 30 seconds. Strain into a jug and stir in the lemonade.

Half-fill the glasses with crushed ice and pour over the drink.
Serves 2 to 3

St Clement's Flip

juice of 1 orange
juice of ½ lemon
1 tablespoon
    Cointreau
1 tablespoon caster
    sugar
1 egg, separated
lemon slices to
    decorate

Place the orange juice, lemon juice, Cointreau, sugar and egg yolk in the blender. Blend on maximum speed for 30 seconds. Whisk the egg white until stiff then fold in the orange and lemon mixture.

Spoon into glasses and decorate with lemon slices.
Serves 3

Milk Shake

300 ml (½ pint)
  milk
2 teaspoons caster
  sugar
1 scoop vanilla ice
  cream

Place all the ingredients in the blender and blend on maximum speed for 15 seconds.

Pour the milk shake into tumblers and serve immediately, with drinking straws.

Serves 2

Banana Milk Shake: Add 1 chopped banana before blending. Omit the sugar.

Chocolate Milk Shake: Add 1 tablespoon drinking chocolate powder before blending. Omit the sugar.

Malt Milk Shake: Add 1 tablespoon malt extract before blending. Omit the sugar.

Raspberry Milk Shake: Add 50 g (2 oz) fresh raspberries before blending.

Strawberry Milk Shake: Add 125 g (4 oz) fresh strawberries before blending.

Chocolate Minty

50 g (2 oz) plain
  chocolate, chopped
2 tablespoons hot
  water
few drops of
  peppermint essence
450 ml (¾ pint)
  chilled milk
4 scoops vanilla ice
  cream
chocolate curls to
  decorate

Place the chocolate and water in the blender and blend on medium speed for 10 seconds. Add the remaining ingredients and blend for 20 seconds.

Pour into tall glasses and sprinkle with chocolate curls. Serve with drinking straws.

Serves 3 to 4

Hot Chocolate Froth

25 g (1 oz) plain
chocolate, chopped
300 ml (½ pint) hot
milk
ground cinnamon to
decorate

Place the chocolate in the blender.
Pour in the milk and blend on
maximum speed for 15 seconds.
Pour into mugs and sprinkle with
cinnamon to taste. Serve
immediately.
Serves 2

Iced Coffee

600 ml (1 pint)
chilled milk
3 tablespoons coffee
essence
4 ice cubes
4 tablespoons
whipped cream
1 teaspoon instant
coffee powder

Place the milk, coffee essence and ice
cubes in the blender. Blend on
maximum speed for 30 seconds.
Pour the coffee into tall glasses,
top with a spoonful of cream and
sprinkle with coffee powder to serve.
Serves 4

Brandy and Egg Nog

*300 ml (¹/2 pint)
  milk
1 teaspoon soft
  brown sugar
2 tablespoons brandy
1 egg
ground cinnamon to
  serve*

Place all the ingredients in the
blender and blend on maximum
speed for 15 seconds. Pour into
glasses and sprinkle with cinnamon.
Serves 2

Raspberry Whip

*125 g (4 oz)
  raspberries
1 tablespoon caster
  sugar
300 ml (¹/2 pint)
  chilled milk
4 tablespoons double
  cream*

Place all the ingredients in the
blender and blend on maximum
speed for 30 seconds. Strain into
glasses and serve immediately.
Serves 2 to 4
NOTE: This creamy drink is quite
filling. Serve in small or tall glasses,
depending on your appetite.

93

INDEX

Almond paste 76
Apple:
  Apple and Calvados sorbet 54
  Apple fritters 59
  Apple and orange flan 59
  Apple sauce 30
  Apple tansy 52
  Date and apple scones 66
Apricot ice cream 55
Artichoke soup 12
Aubergine:
  Greek aubergine pâté 22
Avocado:
  Avocado mousse 25
  Avocado soup 12
  Avocado and strawberry
    whizz 86
  Herb and avocado dip 34

Banana:
  Banana fizz 89
  Banana flip 87
  Banana milk shake 90
  Crêpes aux bananas 62
Beef:
  Beef and mushroom pie 43
  Hamburgers 45
  Steak stuffed with
    mushrooms 47
Biscuits 66-8
Blackcurrant freezies 56
Bramble mousse 57
Brandy and egg nog 93
Bread 78-81
Bread sauce 30
Breadcrumbs 6
Brown bread, quick 80
Butter icing 76

Cakes 70-5
Caramel vacherin 60
Caribbean refresher 84
Cheese and chive soufflé 39
Cheese sauce 28
Cherry biscuits 68
Chicken:
  Herb and chicken liver pâté 27
  Potted chicken 26
Chocolate:
  Chocolate biscuits 68
  Chocolate butter icing 76

Chocolate chip cake 74
Chocolate cookies 68
Chocolate milk shake 90
Chocolate minty 90
Chocolate sandwich cake 75
Chocolate whisked sponge 71
Hot chocolate froth 92
Choux buns 64
Choux pastry 8
Coconut macaroons 67
Coffee:
  Coffee butter icing 76
  Coffee whisked sponge 71
  Iced coffee 92
Cream cheese and pepper dip 34
Crème patissière 77
Crêpes:
  Crêpes aux bananas 62
  Prawn and mushroom
    crêpes 48
Cucumber dressing 33
Cucumber and yogurt soup 10

Daily bread 78
Date and apple scones 66
Dips 34
Dressings 32-3

Farmhouse terrine 21
Flans:
  Apple and orange flan 59
  Prawn and tomato flan 42
French dressing 32
Fruit cake, one-stage 72
Fruit scones 66

Gazpacho 11
Gougère 36
Granary rolls 81

Hamburgers 45
Herb and avocado dip 34
Herb and chicken liver pâté 27
Herb dressing 32
Hollandaise sauce 31
Honey and mint cooler 85
Hummous 22

Ice creams and sorbets 54-6
Icings and fillings 76-7

Lamb:
  Crown roast of lamb 46
Lemon froth 85
Lentil and vegetable soup 16